OCCASIONAL
P A P E R

Simple Models to Explore Deterrence and More General Influence in the War with al-Qaeda

Paul K. Davis

Prepared for the Office of the Secretary of Defense

 NATIONAL DEFENSE RESEARCH INSTITUTE

The research described in this report was prepared for the Office of the Secretary of Defense (OSD). The research was conducted in the RAND National Defense Research Institute, a federally funded research and development center sponsored by OSD, the Joint Staff, the Unified Combatant Commands, the Department of the Navy, the Marine Corps, the defense agencies, and the defense Intelligence Community under Contract W74V8H-06-C-0002.

Library of Congress Cataloging-in-Publication Data is available for this publication.

ISBN: 978-0-8330-4979-7

Published 2010 by the RAND Corporation
1776 Main Street, P.O. Box 2138, Santa Monica, CA 90407-2138
1200 South Hayes Street, Arlington, VA 22202-5050
4570 Fifth Avenue, Suite 600, Pittsburgh, PA 15213-2665
RAND URL: http://www.rand.org/
To order RAND documents or to obtain additional information, contact
Distribution Services: Telephone: (310) 451-7002;
Fax: (310) 451-6915; Email: order@rand.org

Preface

This research was sponsored by the Office of the Secretary of Defense and conducted within the International Security and Defense Policy Center of the RAND National Defense Research Institute, a federally funded research and development center sponsored by the Office of the Secretary of Defense, the Joint Staff, the Unified Combatant Commands, the Navy, the Marine Corps, the defense agencies, and the defense Intelligence Community.

For more information on RAND's International Security and Defense Policy Center, contact the Director, James Dobbins. He can be reached by email at James_Dobbins@rand.org; by phone at 703-413-1100, extension 5134; or by mail at the RAND Corporation, 1200 S. Hayes Street, Arlington, VA 22202. More information about RAND is available at www.rand.org.

Contents

Figures

Tables

Summary

Deterrence of terrorism is best approached as part of a broader effort to *influence* elements of the terrorist system. Although efforts to deter or otherwise influence will only sometimes succeed, to forgo attempting influence because of uncertainty would be to squander the *possibility* of extremely valuable effects (e.g., averting a terrorist mass-casualty attack). That is, deterrence and other influence efforts are desirable because of their upside potential rather than the certainty or expectation of good results. This paper selectively reviews prior work on such matters and then goes on to argue that a useful way to find influence stratagems with high upside potential is to construct plausible alternative models of adversary decisionmaking and behavior—models that also allow for variability. A stratagem found worthless if assessed with a best estimate of adversary behavior might instead look attractive when viewed with plausible alternative models. This is significant because best estimates are often wrong when made about people in different cultures and settings being viewed emotionally from afar. Further, the mind-sets and behaviors of terrorists—like those of people more generally—vary with circumstances and recent history. Thus, opening our minds to *possibilities* can be valuable and alternative models can help. To protect against wishful thinking and other problems, of course, a proposed stratagem must also be assessed by its cost and potential side effects.

1. Introduction

Approach Taken in This Paper

This paper builds on a 2002 monograph (Davis and Jenkins, 2002) and a good deal of more recent research. It has been most influenced by lessons from a recent project reviewing the social science of terrorism (Davis and Cragin, 2009), but also by a book describing the perspectives of participants in al-Qaeda and related movements (Stout, Huckabey, and Schindler, 2008), a book on terrorism and political violence (Gupta, 2008), a new edition of an overview of terrorism (Hoffman, 2006), a book on prospects for nuclear terrorism (Jenkins, 2008), several sources drawing on Israeli experience (Doron, 2004; Ganor, 2005; Bar, 2008), and a recent paper focused on homeland security (Morral and Jackson, 2009).[1]

The paper proceeds as follows. The remainder of Section 1 reviews past work briefly and selectively. Section 2 introduces the idea of using models of human decisionmaking to identify possible targets of influence actions. Section 3 lays out a system model that sets the stage for Section 4, which shows conceptual models of what motivates terrorists and their supporters. Section 5 discusses potential mechanisms for affecting decisionmaking and behavior at different levels of the terrorist system; it ends by illustrating the use of models to help think about possibilities. Section 6 discusses some possible next steps for related research.

Background

Limitations of Classic Deterrence

In the months following the attacks of September 11, 2001, I wrote a monograph with colleague Brian Jenkins on the deterrence and influence components of the struggle with al-Qaeda (Davis and Jenkins, 2002).[2] We concluded that the dominant Cold-War interpretation of deterrence was largely irrelevant for dealing with al-Qaeda as an entity or with al-Qaeda leaders. That classic deterrence concept promised severe punishment in the event of certain actions *and* withholding that punishment in the absence of the actions. In the instance of al-Qaeda, however, such a deterrent option made little sense: September 11 had already happened and the United States was determined to eradicate al-Qaeda—to hunt down its leaders *in any case*. The United States was not about to ease up merely if al-Qaeda promised to forgo further attacks. To make things worse, the rationality of al-Qaeda leaders was quite different from that of Cold-War leaders. Such true believers as Osama bin Laden and Ayman al-Zawahiri would apparently accept a martyr's death rather than bend. For these and other reasons, classic deterrence theory (i.e., deterrence by threat of punishment) was not an appropriate focal point for strategy.[3]

Decomposing the Threat System

Because of this gloomy conclusion we redefined the problem. Our most important point was that al-Qaeda is not a single entity but rather a system with many components, as suggested by Figure 1.1. Al-Qaeda's top leaders are different from its lieutenants, foot soldiers, logisticians, financiers, religious supporters, and so on. Some of those elements might well be subject to deterrence—a theme subsequently discussed by other authors (Whiteneck, 2005; Trager and Zagorcheva, 2005; Stevenson, 2008).

The significance of decomposing the system was soon recognized in U.S. strategy for combating terrorism (Bush, 2006) and is now part of the mainstream view of seeing al-Qaeda as a terrorist network (or, better, as a number of somewhat overlapping networks). The seminal and more general work on netwars (Arquilla and Ronfeldt, 1996, 2001) occurred before September 11, but the concept is now part of the general vocabulary for discussing terrorism (Sageman, 2004, 2008; Rabasa et al., 2006).[4] That said, terrorists tend to see themselves somewhat differently; they recognize that they work in networks, of course, but they may think of themselves as hero warriors in a movement—indeed, a movement ordained by God (Stout, Huckabey, and Schindler, 2008, pp. 33–34 ff.). Terrorism, after all, is a tactic or strategy, not usually an end in itself. Indeed, we limit our own understanding if we characterize those who use terrorism as though terrorism is all that defines them.

Moving from Classic Deterrence to the Broader Concept of Influence

The other major theme in our 2002 monograph was to reconceive the "nonkinetic" challenge as one of *influence* rather than classic punishment-based deterrence (Figure 1.2).

We had two reasons for urging adoption of the influence emphasis: to include all versions of deterrence and to include other relevant instruments of coercive and noncoercive diplomacy that were relevant. Both had precedents in the older literature.

Figure 1.1
Seeing al-Qaeda as a System, Not an Entity

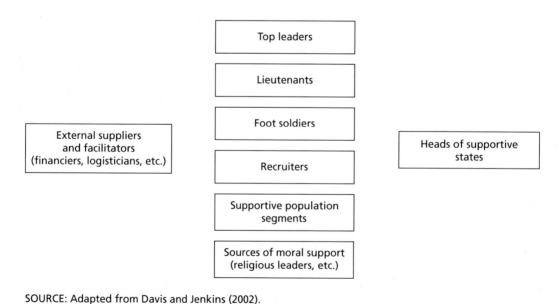

SOURCE: Adapted from Davis and Jenkins (2002).
RAND OP296-1.1

Figure 1.2
Deterrence in a Spectrum of Influences

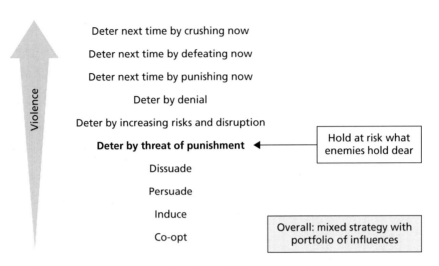

SOURCE: Adapted from Davis and Jenkins (2002).
RAND *OP296-1.2*

Other Versions of Deterrence and Requirements for Deterrence. More general deterrent concepts had been developed during the Cold War itself.[5] Thomas Schelling highlighted the role of uncontrollability—leaving something to chance (Schelling, 1960); William Kaufmann and Glenn Snyder included deterrence by denial (Kaufmann, 1958; Snyder, 1961).[6] Defense Secretary James Schlesinger introduced limited nuclear options to improve *overall* deterrence—by making nuclear war more likely if conventional deterrence failed (Schlesinger, 1974)—a proposition sometimes known as the devil's dilemma.[7] NATO also made doctrinal changes recognizing that even if deterrence failed, it might be reestablished short of general nuclear war (Legge, 1983). Throughout the Nixon, Ford, and Carter administrations, much attention was paid to the special requirements for deterrence implied by the possibility that *some* Soviet leaders thought quite differently than did American leaders and might actually believe that nuclear war was winnable in some meaningful sense. The result was articulated by the *countervailing* strategy (Slocombe, 1981; Brown, 1983).[8] The roles of perceptions and limited rationality were also discussed in depth (Jervis, 1976; Jervis, Lebow, and Stein, 1985; Davis and Arquilla, 1991a, 1991b). In the late 1980s, the concept of *discriminate deterrence* was introduced in anticipation of what was becoming possible with modern technology (Iklé and Wohlstetter, 1988). In subsequent years, various authors discussed extended conventional deterrence and both deterrence and self-deterrence in a world with nuclear-armed rogue states (Davis, 1994; Cimbala, 1994; Watman et al., 1995; Wilkening and Watman, 1995; National Academy of Sciences, 1996).[9]

Regrettably, few of these enrichments come to most people's minds when the term "deterrence" is used. Instead, they often think immediately of classic threat-of-punishment deterrence. This causes communication problems that will not go away merely because some scholars want to redefine "deterrence." It is better, in my view, to use different terminology, as discussed below.

Other Forms of Persuasion. The other reason for moving to the influence concept is that, as indicated by Figure 1.2, influence is more comprehensive than even the broader interpretation of "deterrence"; it includes additional forms of coercive diplomacy (e.g., economic sanctions) and other forms of persuasion that are not coercive (George and Smoke, 1973, Chapter 11; George, 2003). This broader concept of influence effectively increased the battle space in which planning could operate. This was important because some elements of organizations using terrorism eventually rejoin society and become part of political processes (Davis and Jenkins, 2002). That is, even if such figures as bin Laden and al-Zawahiri are "beyond the pale," that will not be the case for everyone associated with or supporting al-Qaeda.

2.   Modeling Decisionmaking to Think About Influence

If deterrence is ultimately about affecting the behavior of others, then it makes sense to construct models of decisionmaking to help us do so. The models should go well beyond the particular rational-analytic model beloved by economists. They should be constructed to help us avoid both mirror-imaging and its opposite—imagining that our adversaries are so completely different from us as to be utterly insusceptible to particular types of influence.

Lessons from Work During the Cold War

One version of this approach can be called *synthetic cognitive modeling* (Davis, 2002): "synthetic" because it draws on diverse factors affecting decisionmaking and "cognitive" because it attempts to reflect the factors at work in a real human's mind (although not the often-tortuous process of reaching a judgment). My work on such matters began when I was leading an effort to build an ambitious analytic war game (the RAND Strategy Assessment System or RSAS) that could be fully automated as a computer simulation or that could have human teams making many of the important decisions. Our Red, Blue, and Green "agents" were computer models of decisionmaking for the Soviet Union and Warsaw Pact, the United States and NATO, and numerous other individual countries.[10] The Red and Blue agents would decide, for example, whether to escalate or deescalate once a war began, depending on what was happening, or projected for later, in that war; they would also select and fine-tune the war plan to be used at a given time—whether in Europe, Southwest Asia, or globally. Our efforts to build the various models were successful in many ways, and we learned a great deal from their construction (Davis, 1989a). Alas for the research (although not for the world), the Soviet Union was falling apart just as the project became successful, and government interest in such work waned in the years that followed. The lessons lingered, however, some of which bear reviewing.

Use Alternative Models to Open Minds

The first lesson was the importance of developing *alternative* models to reflect uncertainties about the mind-set being represented. One image of Red (Ivan 1) was that of the hard-nosed warfighter who would pursue nuclear war with the expectation of winning. Much support for that type of thinking could be found in the Soviet professional military literature, in observations regarding how the Soviets trained and exercised, and in seeing the unequivocal counterforce character of Soviet strategic forces.[11] Another image of Red (Ivan 2) was one of cautious political leaders no less concerned than American leaders about the potential consequences of war, and no more sanguine about the feasibility of controlling, much less "winning," such a war. Although the former was perhaps more in vogue within military circles, there was much evidence for the latter as well, including in studies of Soviet crisis behavior (Adomeit, 1982) and in authoritative military discussions (Sokolovsky, 1984), if read with care, as in an idiosyncratic but insightful book by Nathan Leites (1982, pp. 356–368). The issue here was not which image was "right" (as though more intelligence would resolve the issue), but that governments (and even individuals) can have or move between different mind-sets. Looking inward, we could see the same issues within the U.S. government, so we also had alternative Blue agents (Sam 1 and Sam 2). One conclusion from this work was this:

- In an actual real-world crisis of significant duration, we should expect to see a mix of behaviors, rather than a single behavior such as that of Ivan 1 or 2.

It is an error to assess the adversary (or ourselves) as being single-minded, consistent, coherent, and logical. Anyone reviewing what is now known about the Cuban Missile Crisis should resonate with this conclusion.[12]

Focus on Real Factors Rather Than Math Calculations

A second lesson was that discussions of deterrence and first-strike stability that reduced to mathematical calculations focused on nuclear-weapon exchange ratios were exceedingly misleading (and a terrible basis for decision support). I offered my view of the real issues in a monograph that sought to imagine plausible circumstances in which real-world human beings would actually initiate nuclear war (Davis, 1989b). Such circumstances might include fear, desperation, honor, or a sense of ultimate duty. One example contemplated the commander of a nuclear-missile submarine who had been given a tentative launch order, was being trailed by an enemy attack submarine, and then lost communications.[13] Another vignette involved the prospect of a national leader, involved in a crisis, being advised that an enemy attack was certain and that—because of possible command and control vulnerabilities—"the cost of going second" was intolerable. Thus, the "only chance for national survival" (even if low) was a first strike. I referred to these as *dangerous ideas*—ideas that might include some truth but that were potentially disastrous. In modern times, one might consider the analogy of the "preemptive doctrine" (more properly called a "preventive-war" doctrine),[14] which was formulated with an inexorable logic to be found in both Clinton and Bush administrations (Slocombe, 2003; Bush, 2006), but which, if applied improperly, can be a recipe for terrible mistakes. Emphasizing related capabilities is problematic for reasons discussed in depth elsewhere (Mueller et al., 2006).

In the context of the struggle with al-Qaeda, dangerous ideas abound. These are part and parcel of the religious extremism that characterizes much of the al-Qaeda rant, especially the claim that God demands violent jihad and that the rewards of martyrdom will be glorious. It is hardly unique to jihadis to be willing to die in direct defense of one's country, people, or cause, but it is especially troublesome when the exhortation is for indiscriminate offensive violence and martyrdom to be rewarded handsomely (as distinct from death bringing a vague eternal peace).

Use Simple Models

The third lesson that I derived was that the most important insights gained from decision modeling could be obtained with *simple* models that could be reduced to figures, tables, and a story. That approach was demonstrated in work with John Arquilla that focused on understanding

Saddam Hussein and nuclear "proliferators" (Davis and Arquilla, 1991a, 1991b; Arquilla and Davis, 1994), some of which is summarized elsewhere (National Academy of Sciences, 1996).

Reconciling Rational-Analytic and Naturalistic (Intuitive) Decisionmaking Theories

More recently, some colleagues and I reviewed much of the literature bearing on decision science, including the contrasts between the rational-analytic and naturalistic approaches on which psychologists such as Daniel Kahneman have done so much valuable work (Kahneman, 2002). It has long been customary—perhaps to avoid conflict—to treat the former as prescriptive and the latter as descriptive. That is wrong-headed because some of the most powerful methods of decisionmaking have little relationship to stereotypical rational-analytic styles. Our review and a subsequent report suggested approaches to decision support that drew on both strands of work and considered the strengths, weaknesses, and preferences of decisionmakers being served (Davis, Kulick, and Egner, 2005; Davis and Kahan, 2006). As part of this work, we reviewed first-person accounts by decisionmakers in numerous national-security crises. We concluded that decisionmakers are doing well if they are "merely" able to identify appropriate options and characterize those options for their best-estimate, best-case, and worst-case outcomes. Further, as shown in earlier work on Saddam Hussein, the potential errors of flawed decisionmakers can often be understood in terms of the same model, but with different assessments of and weightings of those various outcomes.

Extending Modeling to Organizations and Groups

It is already a stretch to use models of decisionmaking to represent individuals under the hypothesis that they may decide that, or at least act "as though," they considered the various factors simultaneously. In what follows, I make the further stretch of assuming that organizations or other groups act as though they make collective decisions using similar aggregate factors. This is clearly a gross oversimplification, but it may be useful nonetheless. In reality, we take this stretch constantly—whenever we talk as though our government, the public, a terrorist organization, or a foreign public that may or may not support terrorism is an entity.

3. A System View of the Problem

In contemplating how influence can be brought to bear on al-Qaeda, it is useful to have one or more "system" pictures, such as Figure 3.1 (Davis, 2009a). Reading left to right, support for terrorism (both willingness to join in terrorism and public support of terrorism) strengthens the terrorist organization and adds to its resources. That leads to the organization's having operational capabilities. Support also contributes to a demand function calling for action. Further, supporters can point out vulnerabilities in defenses or become part of those vulnerabilities. The terrorist organization, of course, creates a good deal of its own demand as well—not only by terrorist senior leaders, but also by hotheads eager for action even when ill-advised (Stout, Huckabey, and Schindler, 2008, p. 53). Given capabilities and demand, there will be decisions to attack. The effectiveness of the attacks will depend on the targets' vulnerabilities and counterterrorism activities.

Figure 3.1
A System View

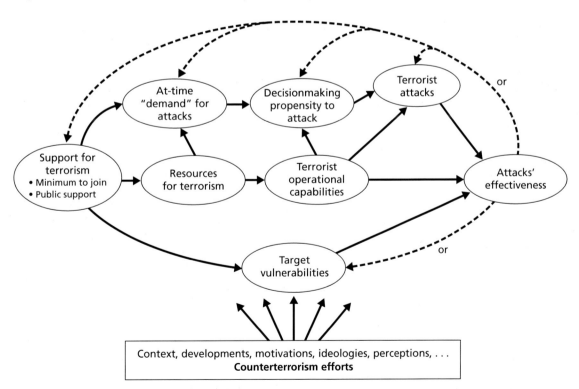

SOURCE: Adapted from Davis and Cragin (2002).

If the attacks are successful, they may increase support for terrorism generally; but they may instead trigger backlash. Further, the attacks may cause targets to be hardened further, they may weaken the ability to defend (e.g., by weakening defensive structures and killing security people), or both. The system, then, is dynamic, with considerable feedback and some conflicting effects resulting in even the sign of some influences being uncertain.

What matters to this paper's story is that the node "Support for terrorism" and the node for "Decisionmaking propensity to attack" are both natural focal points for influence-related counterterrorism. If we know the factors that lead people to become terrorists (or to disengage), that generate support for terrorism, and that influence terrorist decisions to attack, then we may know targets for influence efforts. Let us next discuss such issues.

4. Motivation of Terrorists and Their Supporters

This section draws largely from a recent review of the social-science literature (Davis and Cragin, 2009); it shows conceptual models of how different factors influence terrorism—so-called root-cause factors, factors in individual motivations, and factors in public support.

Root Causes

Figure 4.1 is a conceptual model in the form of a "factor tree"* that gives a first-order depiction of root-cause factors, adapted slightly from a literature review by Darcy Noricks (2009).[15]

Figure 4.1
Root Causes of Terrorism

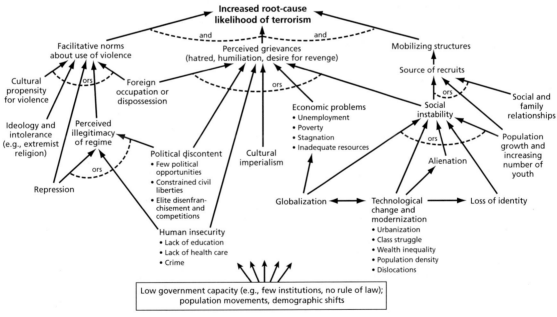

SOURCE: Adapted from Noricks (2009).
RAND OP296-4.1

---

* A factor tree (Davis, 2009b) lays out the factors affecting a phenomenon and may also indicate first-order combining relations by "ands" (all factors are necessary) or "ors" (combinations are sufficient). They are akin to simplified influence diagrams. If an arrow bears a + or − sign, an increase in the factor at the base of the arrow tends to increase or decrease the node at the tip, respectively.

The root-cause factors can be seen as creating the environment in which terrorism may flourish. Efforts to reduce the root-cause factors using "influence" will, in most cases, be uphill and long-term in nature. Moreover, it is far easier to influence things negatively than positively. U.S. blunders in foreign policy can cause a great deal of difficulty (negative influence) overnight. With this in mind, some cautions can be noted, which would be banal except for their continuing relevance and related dilemmas. Looking at the left-most node, the United States surely does not want to be perceived as a foreign occupier; nor does it want to be seen as propping up an illegitimate regime or as opposing a region's dominant religion. It is one thing to express these cautions, but quite another to honor them amid the complexities of real-world foreign policy and past history.

One lesson that may be drawn from history about root-cause issues is that governments that succeed in "defeating" insurgents who use terrorism will find that their victory is only temporary unless they attend to root causes.

Individual Motivations

Motivations for Becoming a Terrorist

The next place we may look for targets of influence efforts is the factors contributing to the motivations of individuals as they become terrorists. In many cases, there is no single decision to become a terrorist, but rather a process in which such radicalization occurs (Horgan, 2009, p. 63 ff.).[16] Analytically, however, we may see what happens "as if" there had been a decision.

Figure 4.2 shows a factor tree based on a literature review by Todd Helmus (Helmus, 2009). Starting at the left, Helmus emphasizes the critical role in the radicalization process of mobilizing groups, which may be either bottom-up as emphasized in work by Marc Sageman (Sageman, 2004, 2008), more top-down (Hoffman, 2008), or—most commonly—a mixture of both. Next we see "Real and perceived rewards." These may range from financial incentives (e.g., for laying improvised explosive devices) to fervently accepted visions of paradise with 72 virgins (Stout, Huckabey, and Schindler, 2008, p. 48),[17] and to more high-minded but grandiose visions (Stout, Huckabey, and Schindler, 2008, p. 39.) On the right portion of the factor tree are the "positives," the motivations. These may be rather in the nature of personal or collective grievances, a passion for political or other change, or both.

Motivations for Disengagement

If various factors can be identified that encourage individual terrorism, so also factors can be identified that encourage individuals to disengage (Noricks, 2009). These include disillusionment with violence, personally traumatic events, weariness, and a desire for normalcy. Research in this domain is relatively new, as noted by Noricks, but two good sources have emerged recently (Bjorgo and Horgan, 2009; Horgan, 2009). The first of these is an edited volume with some case histories. The second is a summary account of John Horgan's thinking, based on interviewing current and former terrorists. One of his important observations is that disengagement often occurs without deradicalization.[18] Horgan also notes that there is much more similarity than might have been expected between those disengaging from al-Qaeda and the much-studied Irish Republican Army (Horgan, 2009, p. 77).

Figure 4.2
Factors for Individual Motivation

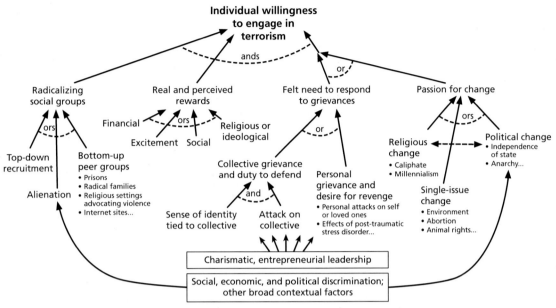

SOURCE: Adapted from Helmus (2009).
RAND *OP296-4.2*

Public Support

Perhaps the most obvious focus for an influence campaign is the public support for terrorism. The importance of public support has often been powerful—both in feeding the rise of a terrorist organization and in contributing to its decline (Crenshaw, 1995; Bjorgo and Horgan, 2009; Gupta, 2008; Gvineria, 2009; Cronin, 2006; Jones and Libicki, 2008). How much and what kind of public support is necessary is a complicated matter (Byman, 2005) and is discussed in a review by Christopher Paul (Paul, 2009); the issue is also front and center in the U.S. counterinsurgency manual associated with General David Petraeus and General James Mattis (Petraeus and Amos, 2006). Let us discuss direct and indirect support separately.

Direct Support

State support is a natural focus for deterrence and other influence actions. Deterring state support of terrorism looms large in the minds of Indian, Israeli, Afghan, and Iraqi leaders. The United States made it clear soon after 9/11 that it would not tolerate state support of al-Qaeda. It then followed up by invading Afghanistan and displacing the Taliban. Subsequently, of course, the United States invaded Iraq—mainly because of worries that at some point Saddam Hussein would cooperate significantly with al-Qaeda, perhaps even to the extent of making weapons of mass destruction available.[19] Another important consideration was general concern about Saddam as a regional threat and long-standing supporter of terrorism (e.g., paying the families of "martyrs" in Palestine) who was likely to break loose as international sanctions weakened. Had the invasion of Iraq and its aftermath been successful, one expected consequence would have been increased credibility for the Bush administration's preemptive strategy (actually a strategy of preventive war).

It is difficult to prove that states have been deterred from direct support, since their actions typically reflect a mix of motives. However, the United States has certainly put pressure on a number of states (e.g., Pakistan, Saudi Arabia, Yemen) that have either cracked down themselves or cooperated in attacks on al-Qaeda and its affiliates. In other cases, deterrence efforts have not worked (i.e., Iran's support of Hezbollah and Hamas continues).

Direct support by a nonstate organization is likely also to be deterrable, so long as that nonstate actor is targetable. Even the Taliban, if it regained power in Afghanistan, might well be very cautious because infrastructure used by al-Qaeda would likely be targeted. It is to be hoped that no opportunity to test the speculation arises, but it may be that the only actors inclined to overtly support al-Qaeda directly are actors that are already maintaining a covert existence.

Direct support by individuals (e.g., financiers, logisticians, security personnel) is certainly subject to traditional deterrence as well as other influences. This is especially true if they are not truly devoted to the cause or if they have family, friends, income, or status that can be held at risk or if they can be deprived of things or opportunities that they value highly.

Indirect Support

Indirect public support may take a variety of forms (Paul, 2009). For example, a population may be the source of recruits, finances and goods, or covert shelter. Even if the public merely turns a blind eye to the presence of al-Qaeda members or affiliates, that may be quite enough. Conversely, if the public turns against al-Qaeda, there may be huge improvements in intelligence—e.g., in tips to the police or security forces, and in responses to reward offers. This is likely to be especially significant if the terrorists or direct supporters are easily distinguishable, as are foreign fighters who have moved into other countries. So also it is not necessarily easy for terrorists and their sympathizers to hide their activities from neighbors in dense communities. It is perhaps easier in places such as Britain, France, or Germany, which have large populations of immigrants and disaffected second-generation children with freedom and mobility. Even there, however, terrorist plots are frequently being uncovered in significant measure as a result of tips to the police.

A Factor Tree for Public Support

If public support matters, then what are the factors contributing to it? Figure 4.3 is a factor tree based on Paul's work (Paul, 2009). Viewing the factors, one may think of influence efforts to mitigate the population's sense of a need to resist, to reduce its respect for and identification with the terrorist group (i.e., to undercut the sense that the group is leading an important movement), and to reduce social pressures and incentives to support the terrorism. That may include reducing the terrorists' opportunities to intimidate the population. The thickened arrow in Figure 4.3 indicates the particular importance of "identification." Another specific point worth highlighting is at the bottom (above the box)—group provision of social services. Efforts to influence public support must recognize that some terrorist organizations (e.g., Hezbollah) provide important services and gain a significant degree of legitimacy (Stevenson, 2008, pp. 54–56). Unless the government competes well against these organizations, influence effects will suffer. One reason that al-Qaeda has lost favor in some countries is that it provides grief but not—so far—services. The Taliban, in contrast, was at least admired by some when it

Figure 4.3
Factors Underlying Public Support

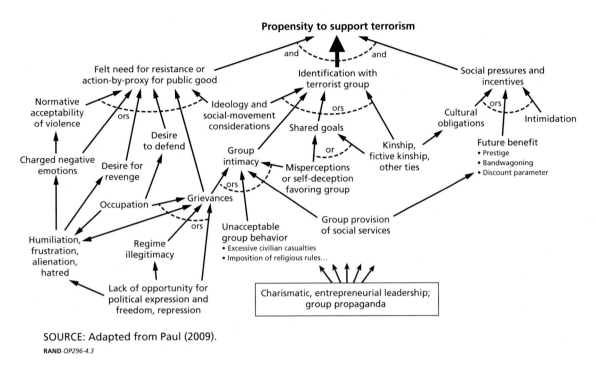

SOURCE: Adapted from Paul (2009).
RAND *OP296-4.3*

ruled in Afghanistan because it allegedly provided a kind of order and security (truth was more ugly, even about that, as discussed in a recent book [Crews and Tarzi, 2009]).

A Composite View

Looking across the previous sections, it is possible to put together a composite view constructed so as to tell a story. Figure 4.4 is my effort to do so; it corrects some errors in a previously published version (Davis, 2009a, 2009b). Moving left to right, Figure 4.4 asserts that the propensity to join in or support terrorism depends on (1) an underlying cause or activity that is deemed attractive; (2) the perceived legitimacy of terrorism per se (i.e., violence against civilians); (3) the de facto perceived acceptability of costs and risk; and (4) the existence of mobilizing groups providing mechanisms for that support.

This factor tree was constructed to explain that those supporting the terrorism are often motivated by what they see as positives (e.g., the need to act against oppression or in support of one's religion that is seen as under attack) and by necessity. That is, by and large, people do not engage in or support terrorism *because* they favor attacks on civilians, but because they see it as either necessary (there are no alternatives), natural (violence is merely part of everyday life), a tolerable aspect of exciting activity (i.e., being a "warrior"), or as part of a religious duty. As for calculations, the tree's depiction asserts that it is more a matter of there being strong pressures or desires to act at a time when the costs and risks are perceived as tolerable (or not much thought about). That is, there may be no conscious and informed balancing of benefits and costs. Those disengaging or withdrawing support may be doing so in part because the costs and risks have become more prominent in their thinking. Those costs and risks may be personal, societal, or related to the cause itself.

Figure 4.4
An Alternative Public-Support Tree

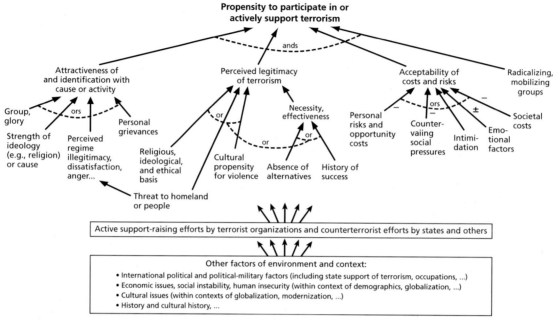

SOURCE: Adapted from Davis (2009b).
RAND *OP296-4.4*

At this point it seems useful to collect some observations in each of several groups, drawing both on Figure 4.4 and the earlier discussions.

Effects of Religion

The attractiveness of the cause may have a great deal to do with extremist religion . . . or very little at all. As indicated in Figure 4.4, alternative mechanisms provide requisite attractiveness, and which mechanism applies may vary with neighborhood and point in history, not merely country.

Figure 4.4 applies at a slice in time and should not be construed to mean that cause proceeds neatly left to right. For example, al-Qaeda recruits may join for such mundane reasons as the opportunity to join relatives or friends in exciting activities. In the course of being indoctrinated, however, they may pick up the strong religious views necessary to becoming part of the organization. They may come to believe fervently even if they have given religion no thought at all before becoming involved. They may also lose their religious fervency if they disengage (Horgan, 2009).

Others, in contrast, may have started with strong religious leanings and heeded what they felt as the clarion call of jihad from local religious authorities. The saddest version of this is perhaps when poor and ignorant school children are recruited in this way by religious leaders in the infamous madrases. Lest we underestimate the power of religious extremism per se, however, perhaps imagining it to be mere pap fed to foot soldiers, we should remember that bin Laden and al-Zawahiri were strongly influenced by religion from their early years (Wright, 2007, pp. 35–45, 75–80). Most recently, the "Christmas-Day" terrorist was apparently motivated by religious beliefs.

Influences for Different Population Segments
One consequence of there being very different motivations is that influence campaigns need to be targeted with different messages for different targets within a population, as discussed by Christine MacNulty (MacNulty, 2008, 2009) and in a study on strategic influence led by Kim Cragin (Cragin and Gerwehr, 2005).

Dynamics
Many of the factors are subject to change. Terrorists may become more or less enthralled with a cause over time; they may be more or less convinced of terrorism's necessity; and, certainly, they can become more or less viscerally aware of the costs and risks involved. And, of course, the ubiquity and effectiveness of the radicalizing, mobilizing groups can rise and fall dramatically in the course of time as counterterrorism activities take their toll.

Cross-Cutting Factors
Some factors are cross-cutting. For example, a perceived threat to the homeland or one's people affects both motivation and a sense of legitimacy. Such a sense of threat has sometimes been much underestimated, as discussed by Robert Pape (Pape, 2005).

Although juxtaposing factors in a tree is helpful for understanding the phenomenon, many important factors are so cross-cutting as to be best shown as, at the bottom, affecting "everything." One of these is the charisma of leaders; others are "exogenous" to the narrow terrorism-counterterrorism problem, as when wars or economic shocks occur for their own reasons.

Taking all these factors as a whole, then, this section lays out a way to identify targets for an influence campaign, and to do so systematically. However, the influencing itself remains very difficult. It is also seriously complicated by the potential—sometimes the near certainty—of unwanted side effects counter to those intended. This problem is familiar as well to those who have studied so-called effects-based operations.

Adding More Detail to the Model

Table 1 is a more detailed (although still notional) model of the ideas represented in Figure 4.4. Implicit in Figure 4.4 is the notion that the factors are binary (e.g., yes or no; or high or low). However, Table 1 allows each factor to have three values, Low, Medium, or High. The table is to be read from the top down (in what a computer person would refer to as an If-Then-Else statement). That is, one cannot read an arbitrary row because a higher row may have already covered the case. This permits condensation: Instead of 81 rows, we have only about 24. The symbol — means "any value" (i.e., the result is independent of this factor's value).[20]

The logic asserted by the table is equivalent to the following:

If A, B, C, or D is Low
Then Low
Else
    If A, C, and D are High, and B is at least Medium,
    Then High
    Else Medium.

Table 1
A Simple Model Extending the Concepts

Attractiveness of Cause or Activity	Perceived Legitimacy	Acceptability of Costs and Risks	Presence of Mobilizing Groups	Propensity to Support Terrorism
High	High	High	High	High
			Medium	Medium
			Low	Low
		Medium	>Low	Medium
			Low	Low
		Low	—	Low
	Medium	High	High	High
			Medium	Medium
			Low	Low
		Medium	>Low	Medium
			Low	Low
		Low	—	Low
Medium	High	High	>Low	Medium
			Low	Low
		Medium	>Low	Medium
			Low	Low
	Medium	High	>Low	Medium
			Low	Low
		Medium	>Low	Medium
			Low	Low
		Low	—	Low
	Low	—	—	Low
Low	—	—	—	Low

The suggested algorithm, then, is simple. The content, however, depends on understanding and defining what Low, Medium, and High mean for each factor. How would we recognize a factor as being Medium rather than Low? Tightening up such matters is always a major social-science challenge when dealing with qualitative factors. Given such tightening, it may be possible to test the model empirically.

Let me now turn to the part of this discussion that is most directly related to generalized deterrence theory—attempts to influence the decisionmaking of the terrorist organizations themselves.

5. Affecting the Decisionmaking and Behavior of Terrorist Systems

An Overview

Figure 5.1 uses a factor tree adapted from a body of work by Brian Jackson (Jackson, 2009) to depict the considerations that enter into the decision of a terrorist organization about whether to go ahead with a particular operation.[21] The figure assumes that the organization exists and has strategic objectives. The depiction conveys the imagery of the rational-analytic perspective, but can allow for many aspects of more limited rationality. For example, the reader should imagine the word "perceived" as a modifier for almost everything in the figure. Also, Jackson refers to sufficiency of information. The "sufficiency" may be misestimated and the quality of the information may turn out to be poor. The model also included such concepts as "group risk tolerance," which may be interpreted with a utility function compatible with rational-actor modeling, or may include subjective and circumstance-dependence heuristics.

Figure 5.1
Terrorist Decisionmaking

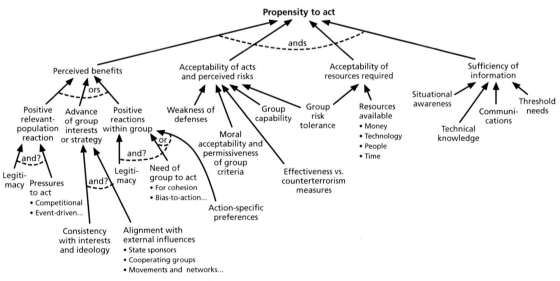

SOURCE: Adapted and simplified from Jackson (2009).

RAND *OP296-5.1*

For the purposes of this paper, the following points are germane:

- The benefits may be judged not through the lens of a single all-powerful leader, but with consideration paid to perceived benefits to the relevant public audience and the terrorist organization as a whole. Does the proposed action advance the strategy of the organization or the desires of the group itself? This is nontrivial, since some members of the group are likely to be more eager for action than others.
- The assessment of risks depends on the defenses (to be broadly construed to include counterterrorism activities as well as immediate target hardening), the group's thinking about risks, *and* the capabilities of the group itself (e.g., whether it has the requisite materials, talent, and opportunity).
- The "cost" of the cost-benefit calculation includes not merely the financial expense, but the likely expenditure of technology, people, and time. Although al-Qaeda has a long waiting line of would-be recruits, it has many fewer capable and accomplished leaders and many fewer specialists in such skills as bomb-making and penetration of security systems, or people with enough local knowledge to succeed in an operation.
- In this connection, there is a good deal of rationality in how terrorist organizations use suicide bombers, the competent ones being special resources to be used against hard targets (Berman and Laitin, 2005; Berrebi, 2009).

Modeling Decisions at Different Levels

General Observations

Figure 5.1 is an overview of terrorist decisionmaking from a top-down perspective, primarily about particular operations, but it is useful to think about deterrent and other influences at different levels of issue, organization, and operation. The traditional distinctions are among strategic, operational, and tactical levels. These distinctions are no longer as neat as they were in past centuries because even the actions of an individual can have horrific consequences, but they remain useful for our purposes.

Figure 5.2 shows an alternative way to decompose the risk factors appearing in the overall tree (Figure 5.1). Like Figure 5.1, however, it is structured to relate to whether or not to go ahead with a proposed operation.[22] The most important feature of Figure 5.2 is that it distinguishes among operational risks (e.g., of being intercepted), the risk of negative effects internal to the organization (e.g., dissension resulting either from ideological disagreements or from members' fear of retaliatory consequences for their families and community), and the risk that the strategic consequences of an attack will be negative even if the operation is a success operationally ("strategic effects risk"). For example, there may be more casualties than intended or more casualties to Muslims than intended. The public reaction, including that of al-Qaeda supporters, may be one of shock and horror rather than one of acclaim. There may be extraordinary retaliation by local states, the United States, or both—even to include what amounts to collective punishment.

Figure 5.2
Decomposing Risks to Assess Worst-Case Outcome

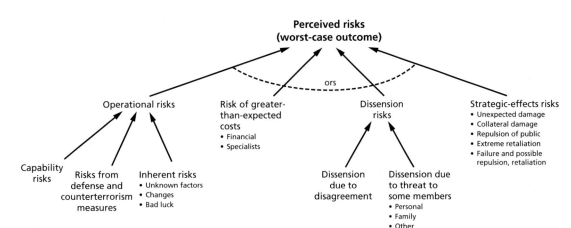

Some general statements are possible, based on empirical evidence as well as common sense:

- Those executing attacks may be deterred from particular attacks by operational risks—even if they are committed to the cause and willing to sacrifice their lives (Morral and Jackson, 2009).
- If enough specific attacks are deterred over time, the net effect may be as though deterrence had worked at a higher level. It would not be proper to interpret that as "deterring further attack on the United States" if efforts continued apace to find a workable plan, but it would be accurate to refer to "deterring further attacks so far." That would hardly be nothing. Would al-Qaeda be increasingly discouraged and reduce effort, in which case *cumulative* deterrence would be working (Doron, 2004); would the United States become more apathetic and sloppy; or both? If time is on our side with the al-Qaeda movement fading, then even temporary deterrence is effective deterrence.

It is also possible to make observations rooted in specific cases and specific empirical sources of information. For example:

- Senior leaders sometimes argue against certain kinds of violent attacks, fearing back-reactions from the public, as in the aftermath of the 2003 Riyadh attack, which killed numerous Muslims rather than numerous westerners (Stout, Huckabey, and Schindler, 2008, p. 54). The public beheadings ordered by Abu Musab al-Zarqawi were seen by Ayman al-Zawahiri as counterproductive: It was "better to kill the captives by bullet" (al-Zawahiri, 2005).
- Those planning specific operations intend them to be successful and often do not like risks. They may proceed with an operation known to be risky, but they would prefer not to do so even if this means delay, diversion, or abandonment of a mission (see the examples cited in Morral and Jackson, 2009).
- Individual terrorist members can sometimes be deterred or dissuaded by knowledge that participation would bring severe harm to their families. Examples of this are described

by Israeli authorities who have systematically interviewed large numbers of current and would-be terrorists (Doron, 2004).

- In other domains, such as drug smuggling, the deterrent effect is a nonlinear function of perceived risk (with deterrence increasing faster than risks). Indeed, that has been empirically demonstrated (Anthony, 2004).

Lest We Be Too Optimistic

Unfortunately, it is easy to come up with counterexamples, such as that some attacks may be deemed "successful" by the terrorist organization even if foiled, if the attack demonstrates that the organization is still in business and has the ability to penetrate anywhere in a country. Nonetheless, partial success in deterrence will typically be better than none.[23]

Some Examples with Alternative Models

Another way to see the potential value of broader forms of deterrence is to use relatively simple decision models. Let us now walk through some examples contrasting the assessment of options that might be reached by senior leaders of al-Qaeda according to two models. The models may represent different mind-sets at work at one time or another because of then-recent developments, our uncertainty as to how "al-Qaeda" reasons, or some combination. Such models can open our minds as to how the adversary leaders may reason.

Each model assesses the option for its expected outcome, its best-case outcome, its worst-case outcome, and confidence that the worst-case outcome really is as bad as it could plausibly be.[24] Scores of 0 to 10 are assigned to each assessment, corresponding to Very poor, Poor, Medium, Good, and Very good. The models differ in their individual assessments and how they combine them to reach a net judgment. Model 1 is more willing to take risks. Model 2 is *somewhat* less willing to take risks and tends to see more risks than Model 1—whether by worrying about the unknown or worrying about whether the consequences of "success" will be more negative than expected.[25]

The hypothetical assessments for Models 1 and 2 are given in Tables 2 and 3. The first attack proposal shown corresponds to the September 11 attack, perhaps as assessed relatively soon before the attack. Al-Qaeda, having studied the plans and discussed issues with team leaders along the way, and having had no serious problems in preparing the attack, Model 1 rates the option highly. After all, the individual assessments assert that the attack will probably be quite successful; *could* be spectacularly successful; and is very unlikely to be anything like a failure because even if three of the airplanes fail, and the other airplane merely causes serious damage to its target, the overall effect will still be dramatic—a daring strike into the U.S. homeland. Model 1 regards anything less successful than that as implausible, as indicated by High in the confidence column.

Now let us consider how Model 2 would assess the same option (shown in Table 2). Model 2 is inherently less confident because it worries about "unknown unknowns"; it gives more weight to the downside possibility than will Model 1. In shorthand, it is more cautious. In this case, however, even Model 2's assessment is "marginal"—inclined to action, perhaps, but just barely. If unanticipated problems began to arise, Model 2 would tilt to a negative assessment.

Table 2
Model 1's Assessments of Possible Attacks at Different Times

Proposed Attack	Best-Estimate Outcome	Best-Case Outcome (Upside Potential)	Worst-Case Outcome (Downside Risk)	Confidence in Assessments	Model 1's Net Assessment
9/11 attack	7	10	5	High	9
Cyanide attack on subway system	5	10	5	Moderate	7
Nuclear attack on a city	10	10	5 (backlash)	Medium	8

NOTE: Scores are from 0 to 10 with 0 being very bad, 5 being marginal, and 10 being very good.

Table 3
Model 2's Assessments of Possible Attacks at Different Times

Proposed Attack	Best-Estimate Outcome	Best-Case Outcome (Upside Potential)	Worst-Case Outcome (Downside Risk)	Confidence in Assessments	Model 2's Net Assessment
9/11 attack	7	10	5*	High	5
Cyanide attack on subway system	5	10	3	Low	3
Nuclear attack on a city	10	10	0 (extreme backlash/ retaliation)	Low	1

NOTE: Scores are from 0 to 10 with 0 being very bad, 5 being marginal, and 10 being very good.

* This assumes that even Model 2 has been convinced previously that attacking the U.S. homeland is necessary.

In this hypothetical use of models, then, *either* model of al-Qaeda senior leaders would have gone ahead with the 9/11 attack. The reason is that both models attempt to reflect the extreme ambition and ruthlessness of actual al-Qaeda leaders, both models are seeing the same "facts" (e.g., success in training runs, and the absence of strong warning signals), and both models are the same with respect to such relatively objective matters as estimating potential damage if an airplane hits its target.

The next row of the tables contemplates a cyanide attack on the New York subway system. The best-estimate outcome is not as high as with 9/11 because of technical uncertainties, but the upside potential is very strong and the worst-case outcome seems at least marginal from a direct-effect perspective (e.g., deaths caused and disruption achieved), meriting a 5. In this case, the information available for the assessment is poor because the security system is not fully understood and there are technical uncertainties about how well the gas would disperse and about whether there are damage-limitation mechanisms in place. Further, a downside assessment should perhaps recognize the possibility of extreme negative reactions by the entire Muslim world (Figure 5.2). Perhaps the United States would have an extreme reaction—even more than immediately after 9/11 with the invasion of Afghanistan. It might flail out indiscriminately and inflame anti-American attitudes (that would be good from the al-Qaeda perspective), but perhaps it would make no such mistakes and the Muslim world—including many segments traditionally supportive of al-Qaeda—would become strongly antagonistic. In this case, then, Models 1 and 2 see things quite differently. Model 1 favors the attack; Model 2 does not.

In fact, it has been reported that a cyanide attack was planned for January 2003 but called off for reasons unknown, apparently by al-Zawahari himself. This was originally described in a reporter's book (Suskind, 2007), which was greeted by some with skepticism, but the account was later confirmed by George Tenet (Tenet, 2007, pp. 273–274), who stated that al-Zawahiri's ostensible reason was that "we have something better in mind." Perhaps the actual reasoning of al-Qaeda leaders was less about risk than about the perceived need to do something more spectacular. The incident, then, suggests that we may need additional models if we are to contemplate the potential range of thinking among al-Qaeda leaders.

The last row contemplates a nuclear bomb being set off in an American city. In this case, Models 1 and 2 are even more at odds—even if attack preparations and technical considerations are favorable. The primary reason is that Model 2 has more imagination (Model 1 might call it paranoia) about the ultimate consequences of "success." Model 2 asks whether the United States and its allies might respond by collective punishment of the Muslim world—perhaps with nuclear weapons or with the unleashing of some sinister disease that would be devastating to the region.[26] Model 2 is less sanguine than Model 1 about the wisdom of an apocalypse or about the certainty with which God will protect against it's happening. Model 2 may also be convinced that the anger against al-Qaeda for making the attack might be extreme and general, including in the Muslim world.

The same uncertainties could have been discussed without mentioning the word "model," but using models adds structure and a degree of consistency and coherence:

- The essential feature is giving alternative constructs serious weight rather than focusing on the alleged best-estimate construct. An "analytic doctrine" that called for creating alternative models as part of assessment, and developing strategy to honor all of the possibilities, might prove fruitful.

Many have argued over the years for something superficially similar, such as having a devil's advocate present an alternative case. The effectiveness of that tactic, however, has often been underwhelming, perhaps because "everyone knows" that it is merely checking a box rather than intended truly to be persuasive. Having the core notion that strategy should routinely hedge against possibilities—even if regarded as relatively unlikely—is more radical, although difficult to dispute (Davis, Kulick, and Egner, 2005).

Thinking Again About Deterrence-and-Influence Measures

Having been through this notional exercise, let us now think again about the value of various deterrence-and-influence measures. Imperfect defenses may look useless to a conservative planner and yet be worrisome to the would-be attacker. Public-diplomacy efforts to encourage Muslim leaders' fierce rejection of attacks using weapons of mass destruction, even revolutionary leaders, might be derided as unlikely to affect al-Qaeda leaders, but perhaps such efforts would be just enough, on the margin, to make a difference. Is there not enough evidence about people in general, and even current al-Qaeda leaders in particular, to imagine that they may disagree about evidence, disagree about risk-taking, and differ about what the downsides may be? Is this not even more obviously true when we recognize that individual people also perceive and reason differently as a function of their recent history and physical condition?

Next we might ask the same kinds of question about lower-level tiers of lieutenants and facilitators, and even supportive elements of the general population. Again, we should not fail to recognize the *potential* value of our efforts, even if they relate to deterrence or to forms of influence that some experts believe are implausible when dealing with religious extremists.

Finally, it can also be argued that deterrence is cumulative over the years and that viewing it as such can be very helpful. Almog Doron (a retired major general of the Israel Defense Forces) argues that case, drawing on the decades of struggle between Israel and Palestinian terrorists (Doron, 2004). He and Schmuel Bar (Bar, 2008) argue that over time terrorist organizations are forced by repeated defeats to reduce their objectives. Boaz Ganor also draws heavily on the Israeli experience (Ganor, 2005), providing a veritable text on the subject of counterterrorism, albeit one heavily laden with dilemmas, as befits the subject.

6.   Some Next Steps

This paper has sketched the case for using simple conceptual models to help guide thinking about how to deter or to otherwise influence potential, actual, or disengaging terrorists and the many people who support terrorist organizations directly or indirectly. Much more can and should be done. More analytic depth can be added to the models using decision-table methods, explicit characterization of uncertainty, and alternative models to reflect different mind-sets. I would like to highlight some particular analytic challenges, however, on which some break-throughs need to occur. These include

- *Adding rigor.* How do we characterize reproducibly the "values" to be taken by the various factors at play? Can these be characterized with reasonable objectivity and consistency?
- *Aggregation.* How should aggregate factors such as "public support" for terrorism be understood in relation to the attitudes and behaviors of the many subgroups and individuals within the public? For example, how much support must exist in a community before the aggregate effect should be regarded as large? How does that depend on the nature of society and various state controls?
- *Validation.* What methods should be used to draw on empirical and subjective information to "validate" the kinds of models at issue here?
- *Collective punishment.* To raise an odious subject that scholars cannot reasonably ignore when purporting to discuss deterrence, what variants of collective punishment, or insti-gating fear of collective punishment, are both relevant and morally acceptable? If such issues are modeled, how can the deterrent effects be maximized and negative conse-quences minimized? Such matters are not hypothetical. The Israelis, for example, took vigorous but imperfect measures during the Gaza campaign to warn civilian inhabitants before attacking buildings in which important Hamas infrastructure was deliberately commingled with civilian apartments (Cordesman, 2009, p. 17 ff.). One purpose was to demonstrate that hiding among civilians was not necessarily sufficient. Discussion of what is necessary, moral, and permissible has been much discussed within Israel (Ganor, 2005, p. 172), where the immediacy and constancy of the terrorist threat preclude avoid-ing difficult subjects.
- *Cumulative deterrence.* If "cumulative deterrence" is an important phenomenon, as argued by some Israeli observers and, for example, by those who have studied the history of the Irish Republican Army, how is it best represented in simple models?

In summary, I have attempted in this paper to lay out the dimensions of a theory of how to use influence (including deterrence) to affect elements of a terrorist system, touching on root causes, individual motivations, public support, and likely factors in the decisionmaking of ter-rorist organizations. Next steps will require a good deal of additional theoretical and empirical research.

References

Adomeit, Hannes, *Soviet Risk-Taking and Crisis Behavior: A Theoretical and Empirical Analysis,* London; Boston: Allen and Unwin, 1982.

al-Zawahiri, Ayman, "Letter from Al-Zawahiri to Al-Zarqawi," October 11, 2005. As of October 2009: http://www.fas.org/irp/news/2005/10/dni101105.html

Allison, Graham T., and Philip Zelikow, *Essence of Decision: Explaining the Cuban Missile Crisis* (2nd Edition), New York: Longman, 1999.

Anthony, Robert, "A Calibrated Model of the Psychology of Deterrence," *Bulletin on Narcotics,* Vol. LVI, 2004,
pp. 49–64.

Arquilla, John, and Paul K. Davis, *Modeling Decisionmaking of Potential Proliferators as Part of Developing Counterproliferation Strategies,* Santa Monica, Calif.: RAND Corporation, 1994. As of March 22, 2010: http://www.rand.org/pubs/monograph_reports/MR467/

Arquilla, John, and David F. Ronfeldt, *The Advent of Netwar,* Santa Monica, Calif.: RAND Corporation, 1996. As of March 22, 2010: http://www.rand.org/pubs/monograph_reports/MR789/

———, eds., *Networks and Netwars: The Future of Terror, Crime, and Militancy,* Santa Monica, Calif.: RAND Corporation, 2001. As of March 22, 2010: http://www.rand.org/pubs/monograph_reports/MR1382/

Bar, Shmuel, "Deterring Terrorists: What Israel Has Learned," *Policy Review,* June–July 2008.

Ben-Horin, Yoav, Mark A. Lorell, William Schwabe, and David A. Shlapak, *The RAND Strategy Assessment System's Green Agent Model of Third-Country Behavior in Superpower Crises and Conflict,* Santa Monica, Calif.: RAND Corporation, 1986. As of March 22, 2010: http://www.rand.org/pubs/notes/N2363-1/

Berman, Eli, and David Laitin, *Hard Targets: Evidence on the Tactical Use of Suicide Attacks,* National Bureau of Economic Research, 2005.

Berrebi, Claude, "The Economics of Terrorism and Counterterrorism: What Matters and Is Rational-Choice Theory Helpful?" in Paul K. Davis and Kim Cragin, eds., *Social Science for Counterterrorism: Putting the Pieces Together,* Santa Monica, Calif.: RAND Corporation, 2009. As of March 22, 2010: http://www.rand.org/pubs/monographs/MG849/

Bjorgo, Tore, and John Horgan, eds., *Leaving Terrorism Behind: Disengagement from Political Violence,* New York: Routledge, 2009.

Brown, Harold, *Thinking About National Security: Defense and Foreign Policy in a Dangerous World,* Boulder, Colo.: Westview Press, 1983.

Bush, George W., *National Strategy for Combating Terrorism,* Washington, D.C.: Government Printing Office, 2006.

Byman, Daniel, *Deadly Connections: States That Sponsor Terrorism,* Cambridge, U.K.: Cambridge University Press, 2005.

Cimbala, Stephen, *Military Persuasion: Deterrence and Provocation in Crisis and War*, University Park, Pa.: Pennsylvania State University Press, 1994.

Cordesman, Tony, "The 'Gaza War:' A Strategic Analysis (Final Review Draft)," Washington, D.C.: Center for Strategic and International Studies, 2009. As of March 24, 2010:
http://csis.org/files/media/csis/pubs/090202_gaza_war.pdf

Cragin, Kim, and Scott Gerwehr, *Dissuading Terror: Strategic Influence and the Struggle Against Terrorism*, Santa Monica, Calif.: RAND Corporation, 2005. As of March 22, 2010:
http://www.rand.org/pubs/monographs/MG184/

Crenshaw, Martha, "Thoughts on Relating Terrorism to Historical Contexts," in Martha Crenshaw, ed., *Terrorism in Context*, University Park, Pa.: Pennsyvania State University Press, 1995.

Crews, Robert D., and Amin Tarzi, *The Taliban and the Crisis of Afghanistan*, Cambridge, Mass.: Harvard University Press, 2009.

Cronin, Audrey K., "How al-Qaida Ends: The Decline and Demise of Terrorist Groups," *International Security*, 2006.

Davis, Paul K., *Some Lessons Learned from Building Red Agents in the RAND Strategy Assessment System (RSAS)*, Santa Monica, Calif.: RAND Corporation, N-3003-OSD, 1989a. As of March 22, 2010:
http://www.rand.org/pubs/notes/N3003/

———, *Studying First-Strike Stability with Knowledge-Based Models of Human Decision Making*, Santa Monica, Calif.: RAND Corporation, 1989b. As of March 22, 2010:
http://www.rand.org/pubs/reports/R3689/

———, "Improving Deterrence in the Post–Cold War Era: Some Theory and Implications for Defense Planning," in Paul K. Davis, ed., *New Challenges in Defense Planning: Rethinking How Much Is Enough*, Santa Monica, Calif.: RAND Corporation, 1994. As of March 22, 2010:
http://www.rand.org/pubs/monograph_reports/MR400/

———, "Synthetic Cognitive Modeling of Adversaries for Effects-Based Planning," *Proceedings of the SPIE*, Vol. 4716, 2002, pp. 236–250.

———, "Specifying the Content of Humble Social Science Models, Santa Monica, Calif.: RAND Corporation, RP-1408-1, 2009a. (Reprinted from Proceedings of the 2009 Summer Computer Simulation Conference, Istanbul Turkey, 2009.)

———, "Representing Social Science Knowledge Analytically," in Paul K. Davis and Kim Cragin, eds., *Social Science for Counterterrorism: Putting the Pieces Together*, Santa Monica, Calif.: RAND Corporation, 2009b. As of March 22, 2010:
http://www.rand.org/pubs/monographs/MG849/

Davis, Paul K., and John Arquilla, *Deterring or Coercing Opponents in Crisis: Lessons from the War with Saddam Hussein*, Santa Monica, Calif.: RAND Corporation, 1991a. As of March 22, 2010:
http://www.rand.org/pubs/reports/R4111/

———, *Thinking About Opponent Behavior in Crisis and Conflict: A Generic Model for Analysis and Group Discussion*, Santa Monica, Calif.: RAND Corporation, N-3322-JS, 1991b. As of March 22, 2010:
http://www.rand.org/pubs/notes/N3322/

Davis, Paul K., and Kim Cragin, eds., *Social Science for Counterterrorism: Putting the Pieces Together*, Santa Monica, Calif.: RAND Corporation, 2009. As of March 22, 2010:
http://www.rand.org/pubs/monographs/MG849/

Davis, Paul K., and James P. Kahan, "Theory and Methods for Supporting High-Level Decision Making," *Proceedings of the SPIE, Conference on Enabling Technologies for Modeling and Simulation*, April 2006.

Davis, Paul K., and Brian Michael Jenkins, *Deterrence & Influence in Counterterrorism: A Component in the War on al Qaeda*, Santa Monica, Calif.: RAND Corporation, 2002. As of March 22, 2010:
http://www.rand.org/pubs/monograph_reports/MR1619/

Davis, Paul K., and Peter J.E. Stan, *Concepts and Models of Escalation,* Santa Monica, Calif.: RAND Corporation, 1984. As of March 22, 2010:
http://www.rand.org/pubs/reports/R3235/

Davis, Paul K., and James A. Winnefeld, *The RAND Strategy Assessment Center: An Overview and Interim Conclusions About Utility and Development Options,* Santa Monica, Calif.: RAND Corporation, 1983. As of March 22, 2010:
http://www.rand.org/pubs/reports/R2945/

Davis, Paul K., Steven C. Bankes, and James P. Kahan, *A New Methodology for Modeling National Command Level Decisionmaking in War Games and Simulations,* Santa Monica, Calif.: RAND Corporation, 1986. As of March 22, 2010:
http://www.rand.org/pubs/reports/R3290/

Davis, Paul K., Jonathan Kulick, and Michael Egner, *Implications of Modern Decision Science for Military Decision-Support Systems,* Santa Monica, Calif.: RAND Corporation, 2005. As of March 22, 2010:
http://www.rand.org/pubs/monographs/MG360/

Dobbs, Michael, *One Minute to Midnight,* New York: Alfred A. Knopf, 2008.

Doron, Almog, "Cumulative Deterrence and the War on Terrorism," *Parameters,* Winter 2004, pp. 4–19.

Feith, Douglas J., *War and Decision: Inside the Pentagon at the Dawn of the War on Terrorism,* New York: Harper, 2008.

Fursenko, A. A., and Timothy J. Naftali, *One Hell of a Gamble: Khrushchev, Castro, and Kennedy, 1958–1964,* New York: Norton, 1997.

Ganor, Boaz, *The Counter-Terrorism Puzzle: A Guide for Decision Makers,* Edison, N.J.: Transaction Publishers, 2005.

George, Alexander L., "The Need for Influence Theory and Actor-Specific Behavioral Models of Adversaries," in Barry R. Schneider and Jerrold M. Post, eds., *Know Thy Enemy: Profiles of Adversary Leaders and Their Strategic Cultures* (2nd Edition), Maxwell Air Force Base, Ala.: Air War College, 2003, pp. 271–310.

George, Alexander, and Richard Smoke, *Deterrence in American Foreign Policy: Theory and Practice,* New York: Columbia University Press, 1973.

Graubard, Morlie H., and Carl H. Builder, *Rand's Strategic Assessment Center: An Overview of the Concept,* Santa Monica, Calif.: RAND Corporation, N-1583-DNA, 1980.

Gupta, Dipak K., *Understanding Terrorism and Political Violence: The Life Cycle of Birth, Growth, Transformation, and Demise,* New York: Routledge, 2008.

Gvineria, Gaga, "How Does Terrorism End?" in Paul K. Davis and Kim Cragin, eds., *Social Science for Counterterrorism: Putting the Pieces Together,* Santa Monica, Calif.: RAND Corporation, 2009. As of March 22, 2010:
http://www.rand.org/pubs/monographs/MG849/

Hall, H. Edward, Mark LaCasse, Robert H. Anderson, and Norman Z. Shapiro, *The RAND-ABEL Programming Language: History, Rationale, and Design,* Santa Monica, Calif.: RAND Corporation, 1985. As of March 22, 2010:
http://www.rand.org/pubs/reports/R3274/

Helmus, Todd C., "Why and How Some People Become Terrorists," in Paul K. Davis and Kim Cragin, eds., *Social Science for Counterterrorism: Putting the Pieces Together,* Santa Monica, Calif.: RAND Corporation, 2009. As of March 22, 2010:
http://www.rand.org/pubs/monographs/MG849/

Hoffman, Bruce, *Inside Terrorism* (2nd Edition), New York: Columbia University Press, 2006.

———, "The Myth of Grass-Roots Terrorism," *Foreign Affairs,* May/June 2008, pp. 133–138.

Horgan, John, *Walking Away from Terrorism (Political Violence),* New York; Routledge, 2009.

Iklé, Fred C., and Albert Wohlstetter, *Discriminate Deterrence: Report of the Commission on Integrated Long-Term Strategy,* Washington, D.C.: Government Printing Office, 1988.

Jackson, Brian A., "Organizational Decisionmaking by Terrorist Groups," in Paul K. Davis and Kim Cragin, eds., *Social Science for Counterterrorism: Putting the Pieces Together,* Santa Monica, Calif.: RAND Corporation, 2009. As of March 22, 2010:
http://www.rand.org/pubs/monographs/MG849/

Jenkins, Brian Michael, *Unconquerable Nation: Knowing Our Enemy, Strengthening Ourselves,* Santa Monica, Calif.: RAND Corporation, 2006. As of March 22, 2010:
http://www.rand.org/pubs/monographs/MG454/

———, *Will Terrorists Go Nuclear?* Amherst, N.Y.: Prometheus Books, 2008.

Jervis, Robert, *Perception and Misperception in International Politics,* Princeton, N.J.: Princeton University Press, 1976.

———, *The Illogic of American Nuclear Strategy,* Ithaca, N.Y.: Cornell University Press, 1984.

Jervis, Robert, Richard N. Lebow, and Janet G. Stein, *Psychology and Deterrence,* Baltimore: The Johns Hopkins University Press, 1985.

Jones, Seth G., and Martin C. Libicki, *How Terrorist Groups End: Lessons for Countering al Qa'ida,* Santa Monica, Calif.: RAND Corporation, 2008. As of March 22, 2010:
http://www.rand.org/pubs/monographs/MG741-1/

Jones, William M., *Escalation Space and Assumptions About Enemy Motivations: Elements in Warning Assessments,* Santa Monica, Calif.: RAND Corporation, N-1269-AF, 1980. As of March 22, 2010:
http://www.rand.org/pubs/notes/N1269/

Kahneman, Daniel, "Maps of Bounded Rationality: A Perspective on Intuitive Judgment and Choice" (Nobel Prize Lecture), 2002. As of March 22, 2010:
http://www.nobel.se/economics/laureates/2002/kahneman-lecture.html

Kaufmann, William W., "The Evolution of Deterrence 1945–1958," Santa Monica, Calif.: RAND Corporation, unpublished research, 1958.

Kennedy, Robert F., *Thirteen Days; A Memoir of the Cuban Missile Crisis,* with an Afterword by Richard E. Neustadt and Graham T. Allison, New York: W. W. Norton and Co., 1971.

Kulick, Jonathan, and Paul K. Davis, *Modeling Adversaries and Related Cognitive Biases,* Santa Monica, Calif.: RAND Corporation, RP-1084, 2004.

Legge, J. Michael, *Theater Nuclear Weapons and the NATO Strategy of Flexible Response,* Santa Monica, Calif.: RAND Corporation, 1983. As of March 22, 2010:
http://www.rand.org/pubs/reports/R2964/

Leites, Nathan, *Soviet Style in War,* Santa Monica, Calif.: RAND Corporation, 1982.

Long, Austin, *Deterrence—From Cold War to Long War: Lessons from Six Decades of RAND Research,* Santa Monica, Calif.: RAND Corporation, 2008. As of March 22, 2010:
http://www.rand.org/pubs/monographs/MG636/

MacNulty, Christine, "Values as a Basis for Deterring Terrorists: Cultural-Cognitive Systems Analysis (CCSA)," *Proceedings of Combating the Unrestricted Warfare Threat: 2008,* Laurel, Md.: Johns Hopkins University Applied Physics Laboratory, 2008, pp. 239–49. As of March 22, 2010:
http://www.jhuapl.edu/urw_symposium/proceedings/2008/Authors/MacNulty.pdf

———, "Perceptions, Values, and Motivations in Cyberspace," *IO Journal,* September 2009, pp. 32–38.

May, Ernest R., and Philip Zelikow, *The Kennedy Tapes: Inside the White House During the Cuban Missile Crisis,* Concise Edition, New York: W. W. Norton & Co., 2002.

Morgan, Patrick M., *Deterrence Now,* London: Cambridge University Press, 2003.

Morral, Andrew R., and Brian A. Jackson, *Understanding the Role of Deterrence in Counterterrorism Security,* Santa Monica, Calif.: RAND Corporation, OP-281-RC, 2009. As of March 22, 2010:
http://www.rand.org/pubs/occasional_papers/OP281/

Mueller, Karl P., Jason J. Castillo, Forrest E. Morgan, Negeen Pegahi, and Brian Rosen, *Striking First: Preemptive and Preventive Attack in U.S. National Security Policy,* Santa Monica, Calif.: RAND Corporation, 2006.

National Academy of Sciences, *Post–Cold War Conflict Deterrence,* Washington, D.C.: National Academy Press, 1996.

―――, *Discouraging Terrorism: Some Implications of 9/11,* Washington, D.C.: National Academy of Sciences, 2002.

Noricks, Darcy M.E., "The Root Causes of Terrorism," in Paul K. Davis and Kim Cragin, eds., *Social Science for Counterterrorism; Putting the Pieces Together,* Santa Monica, Calif.: RAND Corporation, 2009. As of March 22, 2010:
http://www.rand.org/pubs/monographs/MG849/

Pape, Robert, *Dying to Win: The Strategic Logic of Suicide Terrorism,* New York: Random House, 2005.

Paul, Christopher, "How Do Terrorists Generate and Maintain Support?" in Paul K. Davis and Kim Cragin, eds., *Social Science for Counterterrorism; Putting the Pieces Together,* Santa Monica, Calif.: RAND Corporation, 2009. As of March 22, 2010:
http://www.rand.org/pubs/monographs/MG849/

Payne, Keith B., *The Great American Gamble: Deterrence Theory and Practice from the Cold War to the Twenty-First Century,* Fairfax, Va.: National Institute Press, 2008.

Petraeus, David, and James Amos, *U.S. Army/Marine Counterinsurgency Field Manual,* Konecky & Konecky, 2006.

Pipes, R., "Why the Soviet Union Thinks It Could Fight and Win a Nuclear War," *Commentary,* 1977.

Rabasa, Angel, Peter Chalk, Kim Cragin, Sara A. Daly, Heather S. Gregg, Theodore William Karasik, Kevin A. O'Brien, and William Rosenau, *Beyond al-Qaeda, Part 1: The Global Jihadist Movement,* Santa Monica, Calif.: RAND Corporation, 2006. As of March 22, 2010:
http://www.rand.org/pubs/monographs/MG429/

Ronfeldt, David, "Al Qaeda and Its Affiliates: A Global Tribe Waging Segmental Warfare?" *First Monday,* Vol. 10, 2005.

Sageman, Marc, *Understanding Terror Networks,* Philadelphia, Pa.: University of Pennsylvania Press, 2004.

―――, *Leaderless Jihad: Terror Networks in the Twenty-First Century,* Philadelphia, Pa.: University of Pennsylvania Press, 2008.

Schelling, Thomas C., *The Strategy of Conflict,* Cambridge, Mass.: Harvard University Press, 1960.

Schlesinger, James, "The Changing Environment for Systems Analysis," in Edward S. Quade and Wayne I. Boucher, eds., *Systems Analysis and Policy Planning: Applications in Defense,* Santa Monica, Calif.: RAND Corporation, 1968.

―――, *Defense Department Annual Report,* Washington, D.C.: Department of Defense, 1974.

Schwabe, William, and Lewis Jamison, *A Rule-Based Policy-Level Model of Nonsuperpower Behavior in Strategic Conflicts,* Santa Monica, Calif.: RAND Corporation, 1982. As of March 22, 2010:
http://www.rand.org/pubs/reports/R2962/

Slocombe, Walter, "The Countervailing Strategy," *International Security,* Vol. 5, 1981, pp. 18–27.

―――, "Force, Pre-Emption and Legitimacy," *Survival,* Vol. 45, No. 1, 2003, pp. 117–130.

Snyder, Glenn Herald, *Deterrence and Defense: Toward a Theory of National Security,* Princeton, N.J.: Princeton University Press, 1961.

Sokolovsky, V. D., *Soviet Military Strategy,* Taylor & Francis Group, 1984.

Steeb, Randall, and James Gillogly, *Design for an Advanced Red Agent for the RAND Strategy Assessment Center,* Santa Monica, Calif.: RAND Corporation, 1983.

Stevenson, Jonathan, "Reviving Deterrence," in Esther Brimmer, ed., *Five Dimensions of Homeland and International Security,* Washington, D.C.: School of Advanced International Studies, Johns Hopkins University, 2008, pp. 43–56.

Stout, Mark E., Jessica M. Huckabey, and John R. Schindler, *The Terrorist Perspectives Project: Strategic and Operational Views of Al Qaida and Associated Movements,* Annapolis, Md.: Naval Institute Press, 2008.

Suskind, Ron, *The One Percent Doctrine: Deep Inside America's Pursuit of Its Enemies Since 9/11,* Simon & Schuster, 2007.

Tenet, George, *At the Center of the Storm: My Years at the CIA,* New York: HarperCollins, 2007.

Trager, Robert F., and Dessislava P. Zagorcheva, "Deterring Terrorism: It Can Be Done," *International Security,* Vol. 30, 2005, pp. 87–123.

Watman, Kenneth, Dean Wilkening, John Arquilla, and Brian Nichiporuk, *U.S. Regional Defense Strategies,* Santa Monica, Calif.: RAND Corporation, 1995. As of March 23, 2010: http://www.rand.org/pubs/monograph_reports/MR490/

Whiteneck, Daniel, "Deterring Terrorists: Thoughts on a Framework," *Washington Quarterly,* Vol. 28, 2005, pp. 187–199.

Wilkening, Dean A., and Kenneth Watman, *Nuclear Deterrence in a Regional Context,* Santa Monica, Calif.: RAND Corporation, 1995. As of March 23, 2010: http://www.rand.org/pubs/monograph_reports/MR500/

Wright, Lawrence, *The Looming Tower: Al Qaeda and the Road to 9/11,* New York: Vintage, 2007.

Endnotes

1 A version of this paper was presented at a conference, "Deterring Terrorism: Theory and Practice," held at the Center for Security Studies, Zurich, Switzerland, November 6–8, 2009.

2 The monograph stemmed from a study conducted jointly with a team from the Institute for Defense Analyses led by Victor Utgoff. The study was requested by the Director of the Defense Advanced Research Projects Agency, who also sponsored a parallel effort by the National Academy of Sciences (National Academy of Sciences, 2002).

3 Another difficulty with classic deterrence was that al-Qaeda leaders seemed not to hold anything targetable so dear that threatening its attack would cause them to cease. To be sure, some people suggested threatening to respond to further attacks by bombing Muslim holy cities or major cities in the Muslim world. We regarded such suggestions as both immoral and irresponsible, as did the U.S. government. After all, the United States was at war with al-Qaeda, not Islam or the billion or so Muslims throughout the world.

4 However, there are many types of networks; disagreements continue about how best to view al-Qaeda and its affiliates. One interesting interpretation is through the lens of segmented tribalism (Ronfeldt, 2005).

5 Two recent reviews look back at the early literature (Morgan, 2003; Long, 2008). Both note the weight given to fear and the related threat of extreme punishment.

6 Deterrence by denial is deterring attack by convincing the adversary that his objectives cannot be achieved. Defenses, invulnerable retaliatory capabilities, ability to fight effectively at any scale of conflict, and perceived toughness (i.e., indomitability) could all play a part. The latter point plays an important role in a recent book (Jenkins, 2006).

7 A good exposition of Schlesinger's thinking appears in Schlesinger (1968).

8 As a participant at the time, I felt that the countervailing strategy had done a very good job of squaring circles, even though it was criticized by some distinguished academics (Jervis, 1984). I still hold that view. Arguably, the critics underestimated the need to overcome the illogic of our adversaries.

9 A recent book drawing on historical examples also reminds us that some of the lessons drawn from the success of Cold-War deterrence by threat of punishment do not apply well now (Payne, 2008).

10 Many colleagues contributed to building these agents (Davis and Winnefeld, 1983; Steeb and Gillogly, 1983; Schwabe and Jamison, 1982; Ben-Horin et al., 1986; Davis and Stan, 1984; Davis, Bankes, and Kahan, 1986). The idea of an automated war-gaming system traces back to Carl Builder (Graubard and Builder, 1980), influenced by the work of William Jones, who had discussed alternative Soviet models in the early 1970s, each with different propensity scores for war initiation and escalation (Jones, 1980).

11 Unclassified summary discussions in support of the warfighting model are hard to find, but an article by Richard Pipes was influential (Pipes, 1977). Pipes headed the famous Team B effort during the Ford administration.

12 The literature on the Cuban Missile Crisis includes informative but less-than-fully-candid accounts by participants (Kennedy, 1971), White House tape recordings (May and Zelikow, 2002), historical accounts based on both U.S. and Soviet records (Fursenko and Naftali, 1997), discussions of the nature of decisionmaking as viewed through different lenses (Allison and Zelikow, 1999), and journalism. A recent book (Dobbs, 2008) revealed information even more troubling in some respects than what had emerged in the previous 40 years.

A consistent implication of the books is that Soviet and American leaders were conflicted with what (for the purposes of this paper) amounted to be "multiple minds."

[13] This was uncannily similar to the theme of the later movie, *Crimson Tide,* with Gene Hackman and Denzel Washington.

[14] "Preemption" refers to attacking in the belief that an attack by the adversary is imminent. "Preventive war" refers to going to war in anticipation that the adversary is becoming a threat and is better dealt with now rather than later.

[15] I have added explicit mention of intolerance to the factor tree, since that is arguably a root cause (Davis and Jenkins, 2002), although it is sometimes regarded as impolite to discuss.

[16] This process occurs sometimes in a bottom-up way, as emphasized in Marc Sageman's work (Sageman, 2008), but there continues to be a significant top-down influence within al-Qaeda and its affiliates (Hoffman, 2008).

[17] Considerable evidence exists about the significance of such beliefs to rank-and-file members (Stout, Huckabey, and Schindler, 2008, p. 48), in at least some contexts. The belief in the virtues and blessedness of martyrdom is arguably even stronger and more prevalent. This said, it has been argued that, even to more sophisticated members, the theological aspects of the "Global Salafi Jihad" may be the most important component of knowing the enemy (Stout, Huckabey, and Schindler, 2008, drawing on the work of Jeffrey Cozzens).

[18] In part because of this, Horgan argues for effecting change at the social, organizational, and political levels, rather than focusing only on efforts to "deradicalize."

[19] This is discussed by Feith (2008, pp. 491–92), who reviewed contemporary records of debate within the administration, and accords with my understanding. Publicly released reasons varied greatly. More definitive records from all of the various officials will emerge over time.

[20] Such "logic tables" can be the basis of comprehensible computer models, as demonstrated with the RAND-ABEL language developed in the 1980s (Hall et al., 1985).

[21] This adaptation includes moral self-restraint, which is sometimes a consideration in the decisionmaking of terrorist organizations (Jenkins, 2008).

[22] The criteria for assessing risks are subsumed in the implicit function that turns the lower-level risk factors into an overall assessment of risks.

[23] The word "typically" is a hedge. Some deterrent actions could encourage a shift to what ultimately would be a more lucrative target for the terrorists (Morral and Jackson, 2009).

[24] This structuring is documented elsewhere (Davis, 2002; Kulick and Davis, 2004).

[25] A possible example is that al-Qaeda reportedly decided against having the 9/11 attackers go after nuclear power plants for fear it would "get out of control" (Jenkins, 2006, p. 187). Jenkins was referring to claims by an Arab reporter.

[26] It is sometimes argued that such an attack is implausible because disease can propagate as people travel globally. However, biological weapons, such as anthrax, are not contagious. The conspiratorial mind-set that is so much part of the Middle East might in this case be useful.